This sacred thread of love belongs to

Rani celebrates Raksha Bandhan

Rakhi Singh
Author & Creator

Message for your sibling

Write a message to your sibling about your emotions, what this festival means to you or your best memories about the beautiful bond of love and care between siblings.

_____

_____

_____

_____

_____

Publisher's Note

Rakhi Singh's books are a perfect blend of education and entertainment for children, providing them with an enjoyable reading experience and new knowledge every time. The incorporation of fun elements further enhances the overall experience.

In this narrative, the author offers readers an insight into the beloved Indian festival of 'Raksha Bandhan'. The story explores the celebration, rituals, and profound love and bond shared between siblings.

This story is about 3 siblings, where Rani (a sister to two brothers) lands into a worrisome situation and how her brothers rush to her aid, together they find a beautiful and eco-friendly way to resolve the problem and then celebrate the festival with joy and fervour.

It also emphasise the importance of resourcefulness and creative problem-solving during challenging times. Spending money is not always the answer.

Earth Ras Publications

We sincerely hope you will enjoy reading this story. We kindly request you to leave a feedback on Amazon from where you purchased the book.

This would be helpful to other readers who are looking for some cultural resources to teach their children about the Indian festivals and traditions in an interesting way. Thank you!

Author's Note

Rakhi Singh

This story is very dear to me.
I dedicate this book to my beloved brothers – Vishal and Gaurav,
to all those beautiful childhood moments we have had together,
the sweetest bond that we share much more.
I was named after the day of my birth – Raksha Bandhan, a festival
that holds significant meaning for both me and my family.
The dedication goes to the army of my cousins, uncles and
aunts who have always made me feel special and
have supported me in many situations in life.
Much love to all!

For my other cultural and festival themed books, scan the QR code below.

Paperback and E-book available worldwide on Amazon marketplace

Amazon UK

Amazon US

What is Raksha Bandhan?

Raksha Bandhan is a Hindu festival which is specifically for siblings.
In Sanskrit, Raksha means 'protection' and Bandhan means 'bond' or in other words can be described as a verb 'to tie' which concludes as a bond of eternal love, care and protection between brothers and sisters. They wait for this special day all year long.

When is it celebrated?

The occasion of Raksha Bandhan is celebrated on the full moon day of the Hindu luni-solar calendar in the month of Shravana which typically falls in the month of August of Gregorian calendar.

How is it celebrated?

All family members wear new or washed clothes after bathing in the morning. A special puja thali is prepared for the ceremony and roli, rice grains, diya, mithai and Rakhis' are kept in the thali along with a kalash and nariyal.
At the right 'muhurat', sisters put tilak on their brother's forehead, tie a sacred thread 'Rakhi' on their wrist and after aarti, pray for their long, happy and healthy life. Sisters prepare their brother's favorite Mithai or buy it from shops to mark the festival with more love and care for the brother.
In return, brothers offer gifts as a form of love and appreciation and promise to always support and protect the sister in any circumstance.
In some families, it is not only limited to siblings but cousins, aunts, uncles, nephews, nieces, moms and dads too celebrate this festival with great zeal.

Please check the Glossary and Pronunciation guide at the end of story.

Copyright

© All rights reserved.
No parts of this book
may be reproduced
in any form or means without
the permission of
the Author or Publisher.

Earth Ras Publications

Paperback | Hardcover | eBook
Globally on Amazon

Disclaimer

The names, characters and the story
is a product of the Author's
imagination and references from
her real life. Any resemblance
to any person living or dead
is purely a coincidence.

Introducing

*A story of love and care between siblings –
Vishal, Rani and Gaurav*

Vishal

Rani

Gaurav

Rani is thrilled that it's Raksha Bandhan today.

It's the festival of love and bonding between siblings.

She goes to shops to buy rakhi for her brothers – Vishal and Gaurav.

"This time, I will also buy books
for Vishal bhaiya*,
a ball for Gaurav and
a box of delicious mithai
for both."
Rani murmured to herself.

Vishal is her elder brother and Gaurav is younger.

She stuffed all the gifts, rakhi packet and mithai into her shopping bag.

Rani didn't realise that the packet fell from her bag while walking back home.

*In Indian families, the elder brothers are called 'Bhaiya'.

Please check the Glossary and Pronunciation guide at the end of story.

Oh No!!!

Rani was in tears when she couldn't find the rakhi packet at home.

She thought about whether to go back and buy more rakhi's or tell her mom the truth.

Seeing Rani upset and in tears, Vishal and Gaurav rushed to her and asked what was wrong.

After listening carefully to her story, Vishal said, "What matters are your emotions, Rani. It does not matter if the rakhi packet is lost."

"How about we all make rakhi at home together?" said Gaurav.

Hearing this, Rani had a BIG smile on her face.

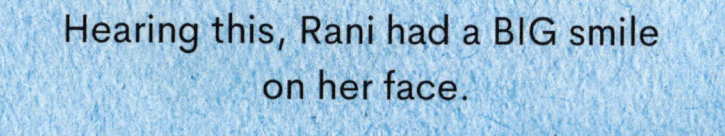

She liked this fantastic idea!

"You go and get some colourful flowers, Rani.

Gaurav, you get glue, coloured paper and a pair of scissors.

I'll get a spool of thread." commanded Vishal.

"Today, we will make an eco-friendly rakhi", he said.

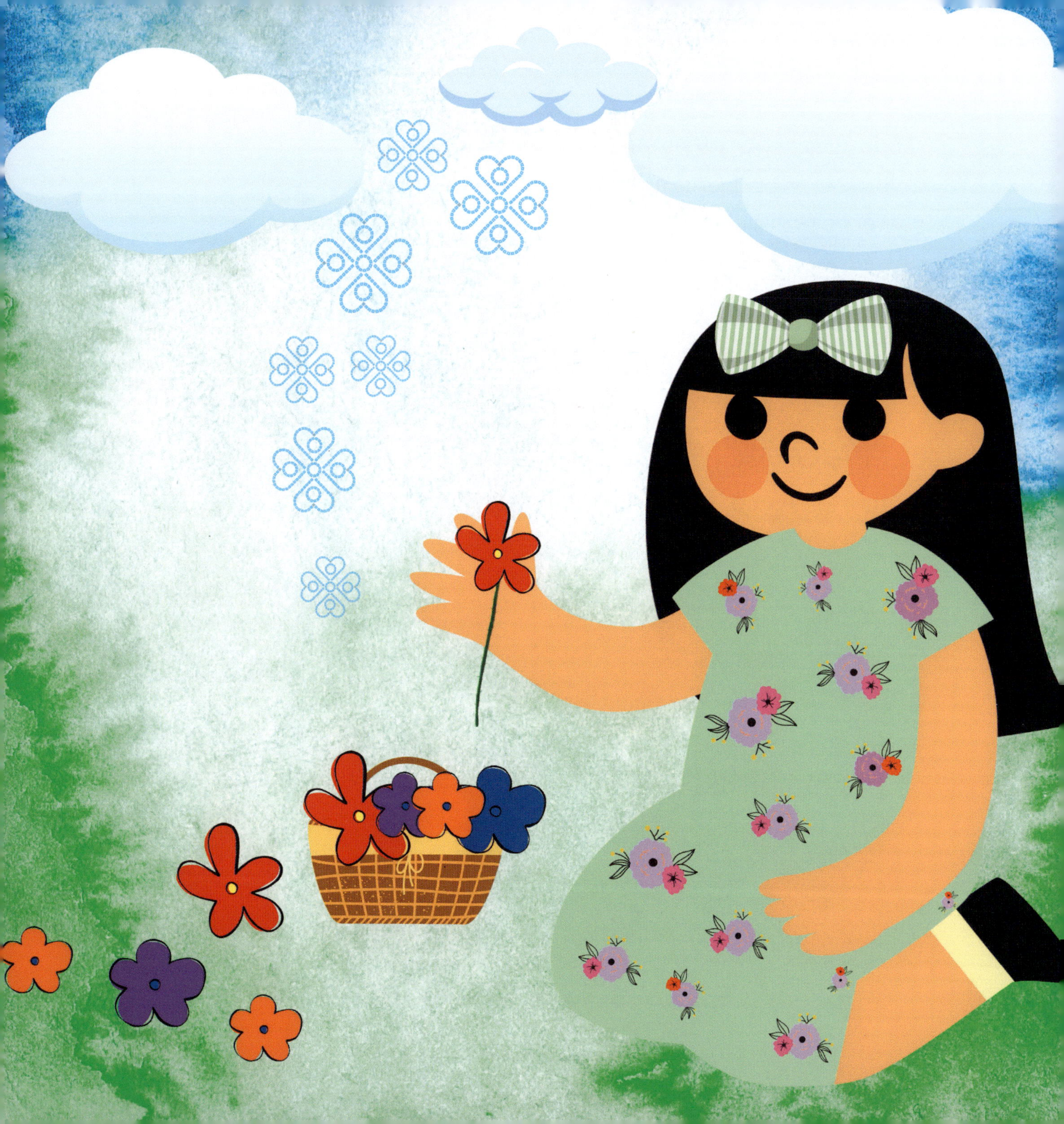

Gaurav came back hurriedly with glue, coloured papers and a pair of scissors. He was very excited about this homemade rakhi project.

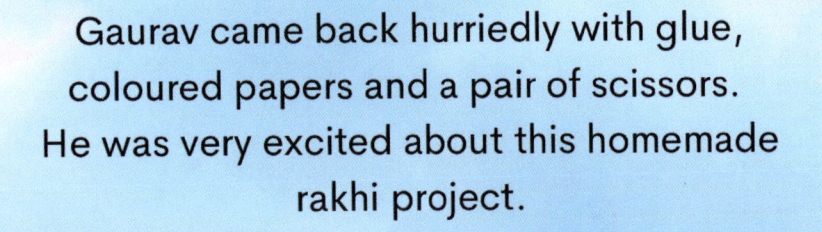

Vishal swiftly got
a spool of thread and some beads.

He knew where his mom kept the rolls of thread for altering clothes.

He then snipped the stem from the flowers.

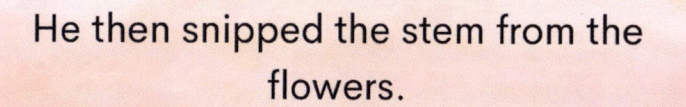

Vishal asked Gaurav to cut
3 small round shapes from the coloured
paper sheets he's got.

"3...why 3?
We are only 2", Gaurav was confused.

Vishal grinned!

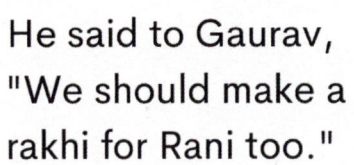

He said to Gaurav, "We should make a rakhi for Rani too."

"After all, it's the celebration for brothers and sisters!"

"Go and get some yellow flowers. Her favourite colour is yellow."

Rani segregated the blue and purple flowers for Vishal bhaiya and the red and orange ones for Gaurav.

Gaurav said, "I will stick all the flowers on the paper shapes."

Rani was not pleased.
She quickly charged, "NO!!! I will stick the flowers on the paper as you are young and can get messy at times."

Gaurav argued that he would do that task nicely.

Vishal intervened and asked both of them to be nice and supportive to each other.

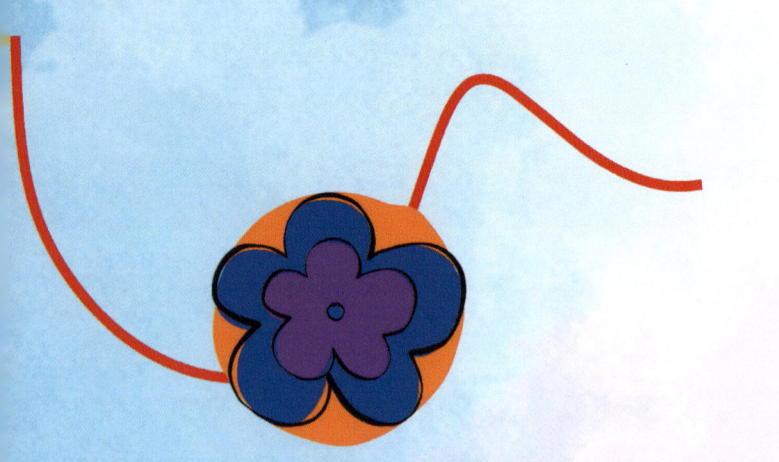

He felt very responsible as an elder brother.

"Okay then, I will glue the thread at the back of the rakhis," said Rani.

Rani and Gaurav were amazed to see how the flowers transformed into lovely eco-friendly rakhis.

WOW!!!

"The homemade rakhi has turned out to be super special," said Gaurav.

"...and beautiful too," exclaimed Rani.

Vishal conveyed his enthusiasm by saying, "This Raksha Bandhan is for all of us."

Mom heard the sound of the children cheering. She quickly gathered the necessary items for the puja ritual, including a thali with nariyal, kalash, diya, fruits, and mithai.

"Me! Me! It's my turn first!" chuckled Gaurav.

Rani did the tilak, then put chawal on his forehead and tied the red and orange coloured rakhi on his wrist.

She did the same to Vishal. First tilak, then chawal and then tied the rakhi.

They all had mithai...it was delicious!

"You both are very special to me.
I pray for your happiness always,"
said Rani looking at both of them.

"Here's a ball I got for you, Gaurav." Rani said, beaming with excitement.

Rani gave books to Vishal. She knew that her bhaiya loves to read books.

Gaurav rushed towards the cupboard and grabbed a box wrapped in pretty pink and green paper.

Vishal placed a tilak and chawal on Rani's forehead, followed by tying a yellow and red rakhi on her wrist.

"This is for you, my dear little sister. It has a necklace. I know how much you enjoy wearing jewellery," Vishal said with a twinkle of joy in his eyes.

"Didi*, I have got some colours and a paint brush for you.
I know you love to paint!"

Gaurav was full of excitement
and uttered
this all in one breath.

*In Indian families, elder sisters are called 'Didi'
Please check the Glossary and Pronunciation guide at the end of story.

"Thank you for helping me out with that worrying situation.
I was really upset when I lost the rakhi packet."

"My brothers are the BEST!"
Rani exclaimed.

"This Raksha Bandhan, we both promise to love and look after you for the rest of our lives."

"Our sister is the sweetest and very caring."

They both said in one voice.

Vishal and Gaurav ran to Rani and gave her a BIG hug.

"This is our best Raksha Bandhan!" all cheered.

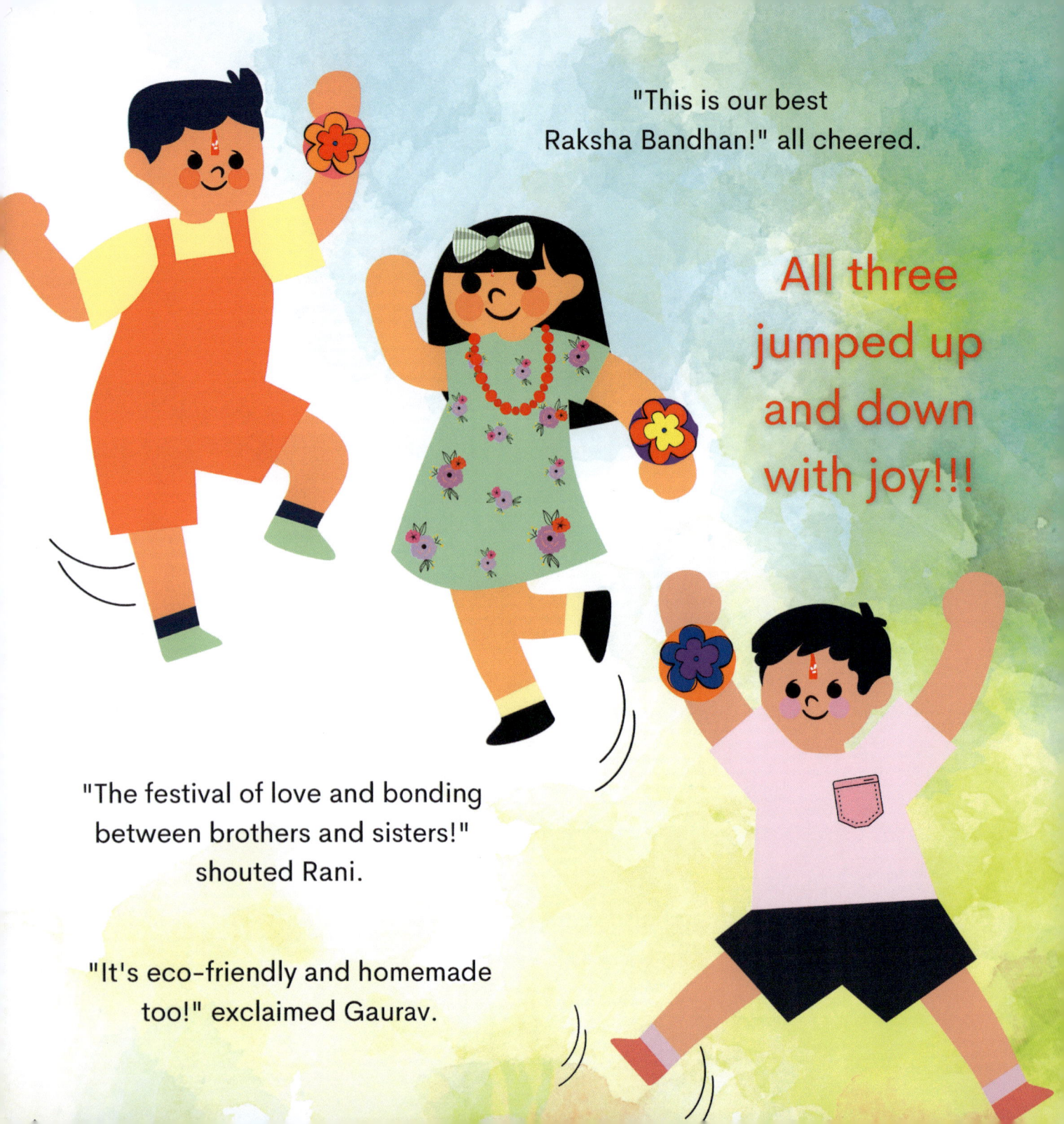

All three jumped up and down with joy!!!

"The festival of love and bonding between brothers and sisters!" shouted Rani.

"It's eco-friendly and homemade too!" exclaimed Gaurav.

Glossary and Pronunciation

Raksha Bandhan: Rak-sha; Ban-dhan (Also called Rakhi, a sacred thread)

Bhaiya: Bha-ee-yaa (Elder brother. In general, all brothers are called bhai)

Didi: Dee-Dee (Elder sister. In general, all sisters are called behen)

Mithai: Mee-tha-yee (Sweets)

Tilak: Tee-lak (A straight vertical line drawn on forehead starting between the eyebrows and going upwards. It is done by a red color holy powder called **'Roli'**)

Chawal: Cha-wal (Rice grains)

Puja: Poo-jaa (a ritual or process of worshipping God in Hinduism)

Thali: Tha-lee (Plate of offerings, flowers, a small lamp called Diya)

Nariyal: Na-ree-yal (Coconut)

Kalash: Ka-la-sh (Small copper or silver vessel filled with holy water)

Aarti: Aa-r-tee (a Hindu ceremony in which lights with wicks soaked in ghee are lit and offered up to one or more deities.)

Muhurat: Mu-hu-rut (According to Indian astrology, Muhurat is an auspicious time to commence or accomplish a task.)

Books from the Publisher

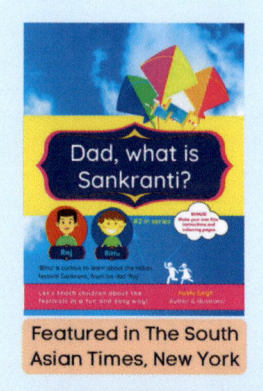

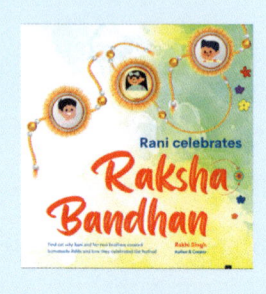

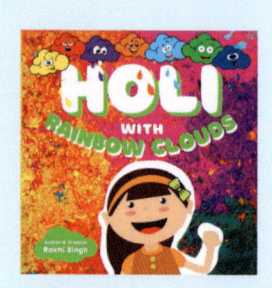

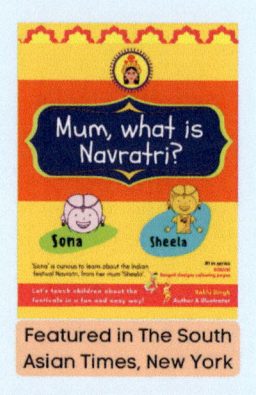

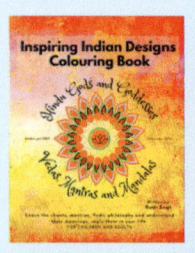

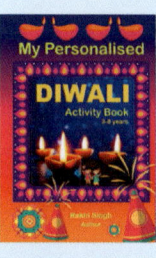

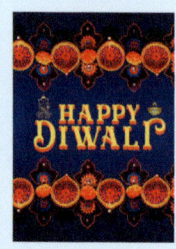

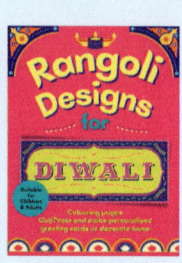

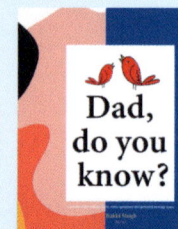

- Dad, what is Sankranti? — *Featured in The South Asian Times, New York*
- Rani celebrates Raksha Bandhan
- Holi with Rainbow Clouds
- Mum, what is Navratri? — *Featured in The South Asian Times, New York*

- Inspiring Indian Designs Colouring Book
- My Personalised Diwali Activity Book
- My Personalised Ganesha
- My Personalised Lohri Activity Book
- Happy Diwali
- Rangoli Designs for Diwali
- Grandma, let's talk about your life story
- Dad, do you know?

Journals/Trackers

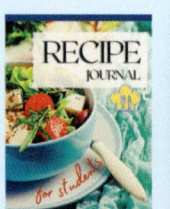

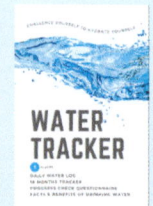

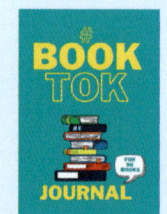

- Recipe Journal
- Recipe Planner For Autumn Soups
- Recipe Book for my own recipes
- My Mind is Kind
- My Mind is Peaceful
- My Happy Mind
- My Happy Mind (2 minutes a day)
- Water Tracker
- Book Tok Journal

Educational Activity Books (3+ years)

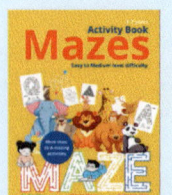

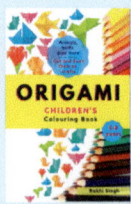

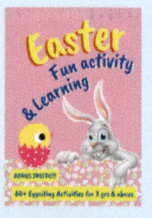

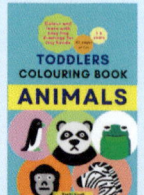

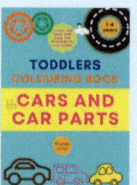

- Mazes Activity Book
- Origami Children's Colouring Book
- Is it Easter yet? Kids Activity & Coloring Book
- Easter Fun activity & Learning
- Toddlers Colouring Book — Animals
- Toddlers Colouring Book — Fruits
- Toddlers Colouring Book — Cars and Car Parts
- Halloween Activity Book for Kids

Printed in Great Britain
by Amazon